DEAR CRANE

Susan Wicks has published eight collections of poetry, five of them with Bloodaxe Books: *Dear Crane* (2021), *The Months* (2016), *House of Tongues* (2011), *De-iced* (2007) and *Night Toad: New & Selected Poems* (2003), which includes a selection from three earlier books published by Faber: *Singing Underwater*, winner of the Aldeburgh Poetry Festival Prize; *Open Diagnosis*, which was one of the Poetry Society's New Generation Poets titles; and *The Clever Daughter*, a Poetry Book Society Choice which was shortlisted for both T.S. Eliot and Forward Prizes. *The Months, House of Tongues, Night Toad* and *Singing Underwater* are all Poetry Book Society Recommendations.

She has also published three novels, *The Key* (Faber, 1997), *Little Thing* (Faber, 1998) and *A Place to Stop* (Salt, 2012), a short memoir, *Driving My Father* (Faber, 1995), and a collection of short fiction, *Roll Up for the Arabian Derby* (Bluechrome, 2008). Her two book-length translations of the French poet Valérie Rouzeau, *Cold Spring in Winter* (Arc, 2009) and *Talking Vrouz* (Arc, 2013) have between them won the Scott Moncrieff Prize for Translation from French and the Oxford-Weidenfeld Prize for Literary Translation, and been shortlisted for the International Griffin Prize for Poetry.

She lives in Kent.

SUSAN WICKS

Dear Crane

BLOODAXE BOOKS

Copyright © Susan Wicks 2021

ISBN: 978 1 78037 528 1

First published 2021 by
Bloodaxe Books Ltd,
Eastburn,
South Park,
Hexham,
Northumberland NE46 1BS.

www.bloodaxebooks.com
For further information about Bloodaxe titles
please visit our website and join our mailing list
or write to the above address for a catalogue

Supported using public funding by
**ARTS COUNCIL
ENGLAND**

Cover design: Neil Astley & Pamela Robertson-Pearce.

Printed in Great Britain by Bell & Bain Limited, Glasgow, Scotland, on
acid-free paper sourced from mills with FSC chain of custody certification.

The tower crane on this site is always left in 'free slew' when not in use. The crane will therefore point itself in the direction of the prevailing wind. This is a safety feature and nothing to worry about should you see the jib rotating when the site is closed.

NOTICE ON FRONT OF BUILDING-SITE HOARDING

ACKNOWLEDGEMENTS

Acknowledgements are due to the editors of the following publications in which some of these poems have already appeared: *Cyphers* (Ireland), *Magma*, *Poetry Ireland Review*, *Orbis*, *Poetry London*, *The Southern Review* (US), *The North*, and *Stand*. 'Explaining Snow' won the Kent & Sussex Poetry Society Folio Competition in 2018.

I am very grateful for residencies at Cove Park, the Virginia Center for Creative Arts in Auvillar, Tarn-et-Garonne, and MacDowell, where a number of these poems were written.

Special thanks to my poet friends and first readers of the manuscript, Moniza Alvi, Mara Bergman, Caroline Price and Jackie Wills.

CONTENTS

Dear Crane,

This morning I look up and you are in my kitchen window cutting up the dark, all fretted steel and open bleeding eye. Too high to move, too high to see your own feet planted in the clay. You look as if you plan to stay until these streets of red-brick terraces can crumble back to nothing, all of us long gone. You lean towards us, stretch your metal arm across. the road that feeds us and the traffic stops, the people in the cars look up. It's early. In an upstairs classroom opposite, a schoolboy reaches out and tries to stroke this craning what, this craning yellow head the wind blows through. What are you thinking? What are you conceiving? Sheltered housing for the elderly, is what we hear. And we are getting old. So shall we be reborn and swing out on your beam, and shelter under you in you know where?

High Wind

It turns the air we breathe to other air,
tosses the glass trees
in the windows opposite, makes phone wires bounce,
our sashes shift and creak. Indoors
lights pull on their flexes like balloons.

Clouds turn to smoke,
leaving the sky cleaned out. This under-eaves wailing
has silenced traffic, children's voices, planes,
till the world is uninhabited.
So much loud air

and no one here to breathe it. So much flying litter,
no one to pick it up. A shadow's flapping wings
have lost their bird, an ageing fence caves in,
a boundary's become
the stuff of thought. I could go out

and straddle it, one foot, the other foot.

For the Blind

At the Co-op door, a dog
sits on his haunches motionless
in black and white, his knotted leash
looped to an iron hook,
each hair combed stiff and hard,
his belly full of tarnished sixpences.

Then he moves his head,
rattles his collar's clip.
It's dusk, the nursery across the street
a spill of light. At the wattle gate
the mothers wrestle with their buggies,
smaller faces gazing upwards half-asleep

to see the glints of eyes,
a streetlamp as it turns above their heads,
a leaf that separates its darkness from the tree's.
They would have known
the dog was real, and never
begging for an antiquated coin.

Now one by one
each street I take goes dark. I walk
alone, watching a patch of white
that stops to sniff under the parked cars
then patters almost silently across
to sniff again, and runs and runs.

Tamar

From here you see it's flowing left to right –
yet pace from one room to the other
and you'd swear the opposite.

Light on the muscled play of water
flecks it with dark and silver,
depth and surface-shimmer.

Willow boles reach down while birds fly up
into a paler sky. This is the fluent place
where world and mirror touch.

Against all reason, we can still believe
what our eyes still tell us: water
is both dark and silver, shallow, deep,

absorbing and excluding light;
this spreading gleam
from a broken branch or pile of detritus

is an inverted shadow. From the sky
the shadow shines, the ripples
smiling as they curl away.

The Romance of Steam

(Spa Valley Railway, 1 January)

Remember the Brighton Belle,
that glimpse of opalescent lamps strung out
from here to other lifetimes
in the windows' glass
as they flicked past, like pearls?

It wasn't that. Yet all the same
there's something about the steam,
the way it swells and rolls below the tracks
and spreads across a winter valley
to disperse.

The way we slipped on mud,
standing to watch each carriage chug away
and vanish round the bend, as water
seeped into our footprints
and filled up with sky.

And how the little bridge still gathered moss
and echoed, voices bouncing up and down
from brick to brick; the way the drizzle
coated us with moisture
till we shone.

Crane

How would YOU describe GOD in One Word?

PUBLICITY POSTCARD FOR LOCAL CHURCH

I tried 'divinity'
because it seemed to show
no prejudice: a category
for a certain kind of need,
historical, a cultural contingency.

I tried 'toast'
because my eyes
were resting on the toaster at the time
and the toaster's shape was retro,
making me remember weekend mornings
lost in childhood dreaming
by the solid fuel
boiler in the kitchen corner.

Then 'mother',
since when she was still alive
I hadn't understood her
and with age I feel myself grow closer,
understand her better,
thinking of her gently with a
you, the way a child might say a prayer.

Then I thought, 'Why *one*,
when they have 'Father, Son
and Holy Ghost'? – and through the trees
I saw its steel-built tower, small red light
and concrete counterweight.
I watched it turning
in the prevailing breeze.

Dear Crane,

Early in the morning when we hurry past, your door's ajar. Your cab's a box of air, so high it's hard to know for certain what it holds. A man in hi-vis jacket climbs your gleaming ladder rung by rung, a yellow Lego man, an ant, a lemon drop that fizzes on our tongues. He squeezes in and shuts the door, sits down above the rows of roofs, the scaffolding. Down there, hard hats, a bed of waiting concrete, a main road where cars and trucks and buses bunch and slow in a haze of diesel. This old school with darkened windows through its screen of twiggy limes not yet in leaf. For seven hours we come and go at his eyes' corners, till he rises stiffly from his seat and feels for the top rung and lets it take his weight. He clambers down, his fingers on cold steel, his boot-tongues thirsty for the earth, and then at last you answer to the wind and no one else, no one inside your head to move your working limb or clutch at something, no one in the glass to lift a single load, align it with its future resting-place.

Feeding the Ducks

(for Robin)

Squares of yellow light
shine through the grey, and at our feet
a flurry of homing birds. A moorhen darts
next to a white edifice of swan. Geese
stand and wait, while over us
this swoop and scream, as gulls
beat the low sky for crumbs. Across the water
something catches; ducks skid to a stop like skaters.
On the footpath spattered green with shit
a goose inclines its neck. I throw my broken bread
and the air is one long screech.

What can you make of this? I press a piece of crust
between your fingers, mime a throw,
but you only gulp it back, a duck or gull yourself.
Your beak is empty, this is your first frost,
you're crying to be fed. I tear off more and more
till there's no more left

and you've become a bird
with other birds, at home by winter water.
You could peck our faces
if we let you, scratch out our eyes. And we're too old
to beg, we only
laugh and hug you, blow on your cold fingertips –
or are they wings? – to warm them,
rooting for remnants in our paper bag.

Driving to Dorking

A man looms at me in the middle of the road
and *I could have hit him.* Then we're speeding north
on the A21, beside the grassed-in wall
of the Medway barrier, and uphill
towards the motorway, its winding glitter-trail
of white and red. A puff of mist,
a sudden bar of light at Clackett Lane
that floats towards me anti-clockwise, shrinks
in my rearview mirror. Then the junctions come,
that web of interlocking bridges overhead
before the mile-long slip road. Suddenly alone,
we're coasting down to Reigate where the traffic slows
to let a train glide past. Downhill again
along the High Street, past the clock-tower, out
by the Blue Anchor, through the wooded dark
and down and round and suddenly a flashing light—
a bike, a jogger – in my mouth
a taste of lycra ghost. Above the roundabout
the cockerel swells its fat metallic chest
and crows in silence. Past the lighted shops
and round the one-way loop, and there
where every week that same white van is parked
I turn and turn again, to trickle down
the narrow cut and point the car's front wheels
across the car park where, concealed
between the plant-hire business and the garages,
we bounce and come to rest. Open the car door
and take a gulp of stillness, see the lights
that seem to shine in welcome, while behind
us in a long recurring dream
the cockerel fluffs its feathers, parts its beak
and crows and crows in silence and it means
it's time to wake, if only I could wake.

Separation Anxiety

(for John)

He crawls across the kitchen floor
and pulls himself to standing, lifts his arms
to me, says, *Nanna!*, and it seems to mean
both me and others who are me
and milk and food and kiss-it-better,
pick-me-up and put-your-cheek-
against-my-head, and hold-me-tightly-
for-us-both. And when he drags himself across
to you and says the same to you it means
both you and me, hinting at what we've been
together all these years and how we'll carry on
till only one of us is left. For now, I take this with us
as we leave our daughter's house, its drive
in almost-darkness, and the alleyway,
the rutted car park where I touch a plastic key
and lights flash on-off-on, and in the doorway
when we turn and both look back
there's Emily with Robin at her feet and Barney
in her arms, and he is wriggling, reaching, wailing
Nanna! Nanna! – crying for us both.

Free Slew

(after Roy Fisher)

On mornings like this
when the sun is barely over the slate roofs

On mornings like this
when people walk these pavements eyes half-shut

When the giant crane's in free slew
unmanned, its metal heart swinging

When another load of bricks will come to rest
and walls rise imperceptibly

behind scaffolding

Dear Crane,

Your cabin windows are smoked green, to shield your driver's eyes against the sun. To him up there this churned-up clay and geometric plan, these concrete mixers, diggers – everything is so much moss and fern, a verdant growth of what? And what comes next will all be greenish – sheltered-housing-green, or car-park-green marked out with lines of emerald or lime, or landscaped-garden-green, leaf green. The paving slabs are green. The water feature's green. The sky's grey-green, blue-green. And even we are green, through panes of glass. No need for lawns or trees or planted undergrowth: as long as you are there our baize-green world is smooth as velvet, his to practise on.

Dear Crane,

Each afternoon at four they free you for the night. You turn one way, the other, turn wherever and whenever, howsoever, stretch your one long limb towards the sky to pierce its hole of stars. A wisp of cloud has caught like sheep's wool in your metal frame to snag against your hook, your trailing wires. You dream for us. You swing on our behalf from one scene to the next, wherever we might look, whatever we remember or desire, your small red fire still burning overhead. Alive or dead, you're burning through our sleep. Occasionally you start awake, roused by your own bad dream – of clay and sand and water, breeze blocks, bricks. A dream of metal feet that plant themselves in earth, and soil and rocks and roots. Of shards and bones that push towards the surface, loads too large for any crane to lift. A pile of concrete weights for which there is no building site, no place.

Look!

He is so high up,
higher than tree or birds
above the barriers and temporary roads
and Portakabins, and whatever grows
under scaffolding and plastic.
High over what once was

the hospital, its rows of beds,
an echo fading in a closed ward,
he touches something, swivels,
makes his metal
beam swing out and hover
almost over us.

How tiny a man is
against clouds, and luminous
in yellow. Yet he sees you in your buggy,
sees me kneel,
and lifts his hand to wave –
miraculous.

You look away and frown:
you've no word yet
for 'crane' or 'driver' – you only squirm
inside your snowsuit till we reach the church
then run for the yellow digger,
sweep off a whole house.

Emergency

You hear them more distinctly than I can –
a helicopter circling above the M25,
a plane that's coming in to land
at Gatwick, concrete mixer churning its wet load,
pneumatic drill a house
or two away. What do you make of them?

Today you sit on your spring-mounted fish
and rock, and give me that huff-puff of breath
that means you're thinking of an ambulance,
and I supply the rest: how yesterday in this same place
we heard the siren, how today
we hope it comes again, that someone else's
fright or toxic shock or clenching heart
will be a small exciting sound
that's swelling in the distance, and then fades away.

Parable

We'd wandered in there just to get away
from heat and sun. By the frosted door
with its clear glass cross
you stopped and questioned me: *What for?*
I said: *That's what they did*
to criminals in those days in that place,
and bit my tongue. Then I told you not to worry,
said, *He was the one*
who was the baby in the Christmas crib,
remember? and you said
you didn't like that story very much.

No wonder you tightened your small grip
and asked to go outside. It was so hot.
But crossing the grass to stand in buttercups and clover
underneath the trees, we saw a little digger
on a flatbed truck. You stood quite still and gazed,
watching the men unfasten all its tethers one by one
and back it gently down.
We saw the driver come and with his key unlock
the steel container shed
where it would spend the night; we watched him tidy up
the tools and drifts of scattered waste
to give it room.

Two Tractors

On the A21 as we drove home
we passed two tractors, each of them

the same bright shade of green, and each
towing a trailer piled

with hay in square-cut bales
stacked up to exactly the same height,

their motion synchronised –
propelled by the same make of engine

towards a single destination
doubtless from a single farm of origin:

a perfect pair
shrinking behind us on the horizon

where they'll multiply
to ten, fifteen, a hundred, in a line

of tractors travelling like them,
their geometric loads

identical, enough to fill and fill
a waiting barn.

Perhaps

'Nanna's not old enough to drive a tractor.'

Perhaps in twenty years, or maybe ten, I'll find
I'm big enough to reach and strong enough
to move the gearstick, turn the giant wheel
and print my U in mud as well as any man
here on the ditch bank, trundle back uphill
in a reek of diesel, mobbed by rising gulls –

and turn, and lumber down, and turn again
until this fallow, weed-grown field's become
a bolt of corduroy on the horizon and the light
is almost gone. I'll drive towards the gate
and turn into the lane and head for home
and see a car behind me trying to get past,

and then a waiting line. But I am old enough to trust
my outsize treads, my trail of crusted mud,
and in my rearview mirror I can just make out
the man who's driving, not in any hurry,
taking in the sight of woods and fields,
the smell of damp on leaves, the birds –

and see him stretch his aching shoulders, turn
towards the woman next to him and start to grin
and shake his head and laugh, and seem
to say with heavy irony that surely anyone
who dares to drive a tractor on these roads
must be the darling of all Sussex

and by then I am.

Dear Crane,

At 8 a.m. in winter, barely light, you're at your post
already, turning above our streets and dribbling cable:
somewhere out of sight a platform swings across, the
man in saffron stands and waits, and beckons, seems to
bless the new foundations with his hand. Grant us a
concrete slab, a girder, grant us a stack of pipes knotted
together. Grant us perpetual growth, from six to four
feet under into human headroom – one, two storeys,
three. Grant us a bank of windows looking east and west,
across the street downhill to where the older houses
cluster, where your early-morning congregation raise
their bubbling kettles almost in unison. Somewhere an
ageing woman sees you take on flesh inside her little
wreath of steam and murmurs to herself, *Dear Crane*.

Dear Crane,

I hear your driver's work is rated as high-risk for heart attacks and strokes (and possibly depression, suicide, addiction?). All morning through the wind and rain I've watched you move and tried to work it out. Is it the way he sits inside your cab, his body motionless, while only his two arms extend themselves, retract? Your beam swings out and out across the new foundations. Just one slip and he could tip a hopper of cement on someone's yellow helmet, bury him to his elbows, shoulders, crush his breathing chest. Or is it how down there far down between his feet his mate conducts him like a piece of unheard music? Through my kitchen windows, over rooftops, here between the trees, I hear those noiseless bars repeating. Do they reach him in his glassed-in cab?

Dear Crane,

When I walked past your gates were open, one of your yellow people bending almost to his knees to wash the pavement with a pressure hose, angling its nozzle between the worn-down bricks – a giant water pick! I looked you in the mouth and saw decay.

Back there you're swaying on your feet. So bite, why don't you? Show us what your gums, your jaws, your teeth are made of, while we bend before you, wash your mouth out, watch your clay-stained dribble find its level, running in the gutter, swirling clockwise down the drain in shades of yellow-brown.

Dear Crane,

Something's taking shape: a whole new floor plan of wet concrete punctured here and there by – are they terracotta chimneys, sending out their wisps of is it smoke into the lying water? Below you in the puddles clouds swim in and out, while men in yellow helmets pace the scaffolding, the sound of tramping boot-soles higher than my head. Something's growing: in the absent walls steel girders meet and cross – from Tescos to Ripples Bathrooms, school to street, a forest of ringing poles, a web pulled taut. A skeleton that slowly puts on flesh. I see a future resident already in her chair, her see-through body bent to something served her on a lap-tray, lapped up by the spoonful, sucked up through a straw.

Paint

I watch the way he plants his ladder's feet
between my roots, the way he sands old paint
like skin till the scars show through –
how even in this rain
he comes to freshen up our eaves with white,
the greying underside of our arched porch,
while here behind the half-open front door
I hide, I try to concentrate, I shiver,
wishing he would leave. The way I make him tea, his mate
a coffee with a single spoon of sugar.
How he doesn't hesitate
to snap the heads off roses to make room.

He must be at least as old as I am
and his mate a decade older,
yet he clambers lightly up a ladder,
stands there on it painting, while the wind
thrashes the bushes underneath him,
filling our hall with leaves. He still climbs up
in his paint-splotched overalls and with his brush
strokes a window frame to white
even as it rattles, filling each nick and scratch.

Over the Old Station

Far below him in reflected sky
a few wet leaves still float;
the cars are cattle standing in a byre
of asphalt. These days the only trains
stop short, the station clock's
illegible through mist. Above our heads
he bends in silence, almost motionless,
to change a lightbulb or connect
two ends of broken wire.

This is the kind of thing
I show my grandson – *Look,*
a man in a cherry picker! Up there, Robin, look!
Together we stand and shiver,
my arms aching, his arm raised
to point, until the workman in his cage
comes slowly back to earth,
vacating his high place
above the supermarket car park's
buried rails, its long-dead passengers.

Two Trains

We stood together on the footbridge, looking east
for what would feel like hours – you in my arms
clutched tight against my stomach, peering out
through a mesh of twisted fence wire, ready to be raised
at the first approach and hoisted like a flag,
until at last I could be sure of seeing something real
and growing, headlights glinting on the rails.
    And when, as we both watched, halfway
between out there and here, it shuddered to a stop
time stopped, as if our lives themselves had stations
where we stood and waited for our other selves.
A flickering of shadows, and by imperceptible degrees
it finally approached. The distance seemed to fade –
    and then a sudden noise behind us made us turn
to find an eastbound train already past the bend
and hooting, glimpse the driver waving,
disappearing underneath us in a rush of diesel,
over the perished tyre between the tracks,
the rotting cat, the bank's wild flowers
thrashing as it passed, until the two trains met.

And now which one to watch? The west-
bound train still shining as it whooshes under,
or the train that came and went so fast
and shimmers down the long expanse of line
towards the hospital where you were born
three years ago, the grammar school
my father went to, smaller and smaller?

Halfway

(for Barnaby)

That morning you pushed the baby toys away,
the pop-ups and the rolling pull-and-push
with wooden beads and twirly flapping bits
of plastic, and you waited
hanging on the stairgate, asking to go home.
I said, *But don't you want to stay*
for all the singing? And though
you flexed your knees and jumped to tell me
Grand Old Duke you shook your head for *No*.

And so I wheeled you out with my ten thousand
down the hill across the captured river,
round the lake in sunshine, all my little men
in yellow buggies fast asleep
under the trailing willows. Whose old dreams
had we been humming? We were down and up,
halfway to something. Far too early yet
to call us grand – but part of me
was at the stairgate, saw the hilltop come.

Explaining Snow

Don't cry, darling. It does that,
falling on a skylight flake by flake
until the topmost balcony is blotted out,
the ash tree all but gone. It falls like rain
but white, opaque – and bit by bit
the grey goes black, so when the sun comes up
it's shining through a wad of white
that melts to tears and slowly
slithers down the slate. But what it also does
is fill the holes, the pavement underfoot,
cover the rot, the crisscross footprints in the mud,
the shit, the chewing-gum, the polystyrene cup,
the weeds, the blackened flower-buds –
and highlight each recessive twig.
Between this square eye and its lid,
look there's a trapped leaf, and green in it.

Dear Crane,

As if the ground plan of our future were a nest and we were newly hatched, you dip your rigid neck and feed us, slopping liquid concrete from your metal beak to fill our waiting beaks, while we gape open, pale and bald and pitifully cheeping as your liquid trickles down our gullets, cools, solidifies, sets hard. No need to feed us now: our throats are strong enough to hold up houses.

Look at you, you're nothing but a wasted skeleton of bird, your ribcage chewed to lace by some rare avian disease. And yet you're dangerous. Your high red light is not to tell us your steel frame's inhabited; it's there to warn us. We could stumble, totter, blunder into you. Or something from the sky above our heads could wrap its flaming body round your spine and bring you back to life, your yellow bones lit up, your girders melting, sagging, oozing gold, imagine, making you great again. Sometimes in the dark your light's the only thing we see. Sometimes in the fog your high red eye is kind enough to draw a veil.

Dear Crane,

When I looked out at six, you'd disappeared into the cloud, a blankness where your body was. Where your beam swung out there's nothing but this flat grey which could be sky or dirty cotton wool or setting concrete. Or a wall of styrofoam where screams are silenced. Or a mask, a veil, a game, a sleight of hand, a slight. You could be testing us. You could just be impervious. Okay, I get it: each of us peers out alone through fog and sees no other house. So sling your dangling hook, why don't you? I for one won't miss your bony skeleton, your overweening height, your red eye winking nonchalant across a roof. Who fucking cares? And then, about eleven, you appear.

Dear Crane,

They've rolled you out a brand-new apron stage of tarmac, where the workmen in their goggles and hard hats can come and take their bows. I almost clap. They've learnt their parts so well, they've blocked their movements out, rehearsed each scene for weeks: no one will dry or corpse. A stack of iron lattice dangles on its metal thread and someone waves it down. We stand and watch. What a performance! So well done we hardly see it move as high above us all you swivel without swivelling. The cold has numbed our hands. Perhaps our lives will never be enough to see the whole production. Yet the tarmac apron's here, the scaffolding. Those hard hats bobbing there above the metal poles are word and gesture perfect, and their dance is tragic, comic. Maybe we should satisfy ourselves with this and praise you anyway and put our hands together just for warmth, why not? There's nothing lost.

Dear Crane,

So here we are. The frontage of one block is almost there, the second block a bare design on concrete with a hint of scaffolding. Between them you stand motionless. You're weighing up your options. Finish what is almost finished? Start again? Already the first block has walls and window spaces. Yellow jackets buzz about their business, that much farther from the ground. Should you incline yourself towards the gateway where those piles of strapped-together roof tiles lie in waiting? Should you bend this way to lift these bundled poles and make another scaffold? Which do you love most, the breeze blocks or the breeze? And don't you think enough old people people your pummelled patch already, do you really need to build a house to house a hundred more? If we're to be among them, couldn't you lift just us without this fuss, eliminate the middle-man, the plans, the whole concomitant construction – raise *us* to the sky on your steel tray, then suddenly release the cable, clanking like a shout?

Stacked Planes, 5.30 a.m.

Their wings dip gravely sideways
level off I almost hear them turning
and then dip again
like angels on a ladder every revolution
one rung lower   under my own ceiling
I can almost see the
blinking lights the passengers half–
sleeping all that baggage
stowed in the overhead lockers under–
neath their feet their shoulders aching
as they lean to a small window
try to catch a glimpse of
something they might recognise a
motorway for instance or a reservoir
a silver lizard or the Channel
edged with lace   and I
am half–asleep myself and almost
praying
           Let them
see it all in gleaming black and white
the way we used to
in the photographs you gave us
when we learned to read an O.S. map
and place ourselves
here at the edge of an old wood or
here on the far bank
of a forgotten railway cutting or just here
in boots and ready on this path
to travel either way as soon
as sun comes creeping over the horizon
casting giant shadows
and they let the aircraft turn

one final time and
point the nose towards the runway
let the wheels come down.

Dicky Ticker

(i.m. G.H.)

You wrote it in an email to my husband
from some inner country farther off
than Germany
             as if from some dark war
long gone – but I can see you as you were
when we first met –
               your gangly body
in a rainbow sweater, your mop-head of hair
behind the glasses – and yourself
still laughing,
             Love's *Forever Changes*
clutched like a vinyl breastplate to your chest.

You were the sideways one,
                 the not-quite-there,
the thigh-slap, eager-to-be-gone, too-bored-to-linger.
You were always off
             towards the next free ride,
the next 'real coup', the bunch of fruit
that landed in your lap.
             I almost lost
my summer job because of you – you wouldn't ever
             buckle under, pelted me
with raspberries between the canes
while listening to the Test Match on a small transistor –
mine!

   Yet you were the one who stayed
and I came South. The note you wrote me then
still makes me weep. I hardly recognise
the boy I thought I knew.

But this one, yes,
the *dicky ticker*,
        yes, I hear you – you're still there
in your grandpa's old-world slang, that half-ironic tongue
of half-escape,
        of distance-making-safe –
                the child you were
abandoned by his mother, left to learn
the lingo of her parents.
        Now in memory
I hear that soundtrack sung by Love.
I note the date you died, and hear
an old clock wheezing
        as it clears its throat.

Midwich Cuckoo

(after John Wyndham)

I read it on my camp-bed in our kitchen
on a day my nanna 'wasn't quite herself',
when she'd talked all night. Between the pages
I can still smell canvas, feel the wooden frame
behind my knees, the quarry tiles
still cold in sunlight slanting from the garden.
That was my 'day out'
from school – for what? I wasn't sick exactly,
only frightened, fifteen, hiding
inside that transparent dome, where everyone
was either dead or sleeping – till the world
eventually awoke and all the women –
even virgins, even the unmarried! –
found themselves 'with child'. I *was*
that child, a gold-eyed Eric or Priscilla,
asking to survive and ruthless,
sharing every thought: together
we would find my life, my clothes, my bedroom
where my nanna's voice had finally gone quiet
and at any moment Doctor Hughes would come
with an official letter and they'd drive her
down to Netherne. I would find an explanation
for that last crusade, the villagers
at one another's throats or slavering,
the impulse that could make a pilot and his crew
bale out on parachutes and float to earth
in safety while their unmanned plane flew on.

M25

When we were travelling this road
to fetch our grandson
while our daughter waited to give birth,
the Downs were streaked with sunlight, green and gold,
the January trees were puffs of haze,
transparent. Catkins released their pollen in a cloud.

And then, when we drove west
to meet his little brother, he was in his seat
behind us, while you steered
uphill towards the Downs, the air
full of wet snow, the stars of flakes
fluttering through our headlights, lit from underneath.

Now, as you drive the same way alone
a truck comes inching in
closer and closer, clips your nearside wing
and almost sends you spinning. Now the lanes
are clotted red with light – our children and grandchildren
travel on without us. Oh, my darling.

The Old Cemetery, Cove

Le vent se lève. Il faut tenter de vivre.

PAUL VALÉRY,
'Le Cimetière marin'

Four-twenty in the afternoon, it's much too late
to measure sun and shadows. Below me in a salty gleam
a tanker's going out, a submarine
is nosing at the underlife of seas, a yacht
is making for harbour before dusk. The graves
look cared-for, polished; even the craggiest old lumps
belie their age. Between the acers and the yews' dark,
a snatch of water, mountain, clouds – it is too beautiful
to lie here dead in. On this slick of hillside
even unbelievers put their best foot forward,
wrap themselves in turf between the fog's soft fingers,
where the far shore appears and disappears.

*

It's almost time for me to leave. Above my head
the turf is wet. Across the surface of a pond
no rings but motion spreading from a centre – I have never
seen the Loch as rough as this, the day's flat silver
lashed to leaping white I wouldn't call them sheep
as Frenchmen do or horses, but the wind
is blowing and the water's slate
is new and empty, quick
with something leaping, something catching light.

Dear Crane,

Until today I never knew how far your image reached. Cresting the brow of a hill four miles away I saw you, higher than us all. Across the maze of tight-packed streets I looked and you were there, a plane caught in your spine. And you looked back. I see you from the supermarket door as I lug home my bags of milk and vegetables. I see you from the park and everything goes small, the children on the slide abandoned, dogs unclipped from leashes scuttling round like bugs. And even from the pool I see you pointing skyward as I swim – one stroke, another stroke, a length, or two or ten or thirty lengths and turn and there you are, far off, encased in glass, still with me, one arm lunging strongly, keeping pace.

Dear Crane,

Spiking our cities, right across the surface of the globe your other selves are working – standing, swinging, dipping, rising, swivelling out of sync. In a distant foreign town a workman shouts. A child looks up and points. A mother feels a pulling on her arm and struggles to move on. And it's impossible. You're striding like a War of Worlds across our brown-field land, you've occupied our towns, the future's everywhere we look. You loom at every window, posing for a selfie on a cloth of stars. You've hypnotised our young. And now there's nothing we can hold or save or teach them: they're the ones insisting that we stand to watch you as your giant shadow falls across their hands.

Dear Crane,

Your red eye's blinking at me, off and on, through leaves, through air, and suddenly I notice you've been naked all these months. Now for the first time I'm seeing you in lace, the palest green. It must be spring. A pity. You were better bare, when what we saw was what you really were.

The winter was your spiritual season – skies of heavy cloud, or pale, the odd bare branch, the windows opposite your site all shut. Spring makes you sheepish. Can a crane feel shame? You shouldn't. We'll get used to this gold green, and you wear it well. Soon summer covers you with dust, the buildings at your feet will clamber to your knees and start to steal your views.

Your time is limited. Before you know it, autumn will have come again to fill the steel net of your body with its flying shadows and migrations, fungus-spotted leaves.

Clubbercise

It's a kind of keeping fit, apparently: they move
in unison in darkness, only the bright tips
of their glow-sticks glowing white
or blue or green, while their reflection in the mirrors
is a single underwater creature reaching,
growing as I watch. I stand
where God would stand, admiring His creation
and its strangeness, though this is no sea-bed,
and the eyes that watch not God's
and I am thinking not of gods or monsters or creation
but of how my father used to take us every year to Croydon
to the Grand, to see the pantomime, and how we
drank it in, the *Look-out-he's-behind-you!*
and the trapdoor puff of smoke, the choruses.
And then that moment we'd been waiting for all evening
when the lights went out
and there on stage they'd start to dance in darkness –
butterflies with phosphorescent wings
or fish or birds or flower-petals,
skeletons that rattled their long bones
in white on black – and we were
rapt and barely breathing,
too caught up to see the dangling ropes. And we were
with them as they flew or swam or scattered,
clashed their pelvises
like human castanets, and dancing
meant exactly this. And growing, fledging, dying
were a shifting pattern you could
watch one day a year, and not forget.

Elderly Bathing Solutions

(after an online advertisement)

They used to be blue or pink, a foil-wrapped cube
dissolved in water, crumbling bit by bit.

Or out of a small bottle, creamed with coconut
or lanolin; that crystal gel in half-transparent beads

that swam away, avoiding the hot tap
to glitter like a shoal of little fish

and surface in a drift of bubbles at the far end.
Now they are almost colourless,

even their labels faded. When I unscrew the cap,
upend the bottle, nothing. They are so old

they cannot be decanted. We must learn to bathe
in milk, Prosecco, Guinness, mud,

or let the hungry fishes nibble at the dead
of our bare soles – or simply break

the glass and mix them all together, shake
and then dilute them, reimagine them as young.

Rhubarb

Twice a year it does its phoenix act,
the long stems shooting up and shining
red or pink in sun like fingers
closed on a lit torch.

In there under the leaves
is something that dies back
and comes again, and dies, and waits
for rain. Sometimes so many stems

you're spoilt for choice; sometimes
so few you pull out all there is.
Not like my parents' older, deeper roots
at the foot of that steep climb

slimy with moss, which never
gave out once. They said those tiny fists
of coming leaves were poisonous
if eaten raw; the coral nib

at the earth end of each stalk
was sheathed with death. No one was sure.
We picked them anyway and sucked,
checking that sour was sour.

Maine, End of Summer

At first the islands crawled out of the deep
peasouper, rested, then crawled back
inside a broth of shapes, condensed to drops
that sounded on the corrugated metal roof
of the low porch. A fleet of lobster boats
went chugging through our sleep.

But something happened that first Sunday
lunch with you and Persis and her old Maine friends –
those soft-shell lobsters we could prise apart
with thumbs and fingers in a sudden spurt
of juices, and the liver's green moraine,
the legs like spiders', tails that came out clean.

The way we sat together at the outdoor table
under that ringing roof. How Ike unblocked
the upstairs toilet with a tool he called a snake
as we stood round and watched.
How afterwards I wandered through the house
looking at all the photos, that old Ancient

Mariner engraving pinned beneath the stairs
while under us the lobsters crawled like shadows,
pincers blushing, half-bared by the tide.
How after that the mist dissolved to give
a week of sun, and leaves blazed silently
to coral, burgundy or lobster as they died.

After the Lobster Feast

(South Bristol, Maine)

When we'd yawned and stretched and cleared the carapaces
all those heart-finned tails and gauntlet claws
and bowls of melted butter with their greenish smears
of soft delicious liver and the crumpled
packets full of nothing but a few remaining splinters
and the other guests had gone we paused
for breath and sat about and talked among ourselves
as one by one the islands that had made themselves that morning
out of mist in a narrow gleam of sun
were gradually sucked back across the non-
horizon. Just above the shoreline
where we'd watched a fledgling eagle settle gorging on a duck
the rock was swallowed up. We lingered
sitting on the porch swing emptying our glasses
talking in low voices till some throwaway remark
made Ken get out his laptop *Yeah, I know the one –*
Debussy's Cathédrale engloutie and I think I raised my hand,
Don't turn it off, please leave it – leave the music playing
tinnily from nowhere into nowhere no one even listening
but the long-departed cousins of his childhood
or the unsubstantiated islands
while the gaping shells and claws he'd thrown back to the ocean
floated in the darkness rocking, drawn towards the sound.

Dear Crane,

Do you feel cold, with human habitations crowding at your spine? Do spots of rust stand up like gooseflesh on your skin? Before too long you'll stretch your arm across the surface of a slick new roof and start to shiver, tilt and be swept under, one last glimpse of concrete mixer turning, one last gulp of sky. One morning early, when the traffic's scarcely flowing, they will load you on a giant truck and take you who knows where. How can I make you see how needed you still are? Your small red light blinks through the swaying branches, brighter than brickwork, wiser than human wish. If I were you I'd take this chance to swing with every breath. I'd slew myself full-circle in a last goodbye.

Dear Crane,

When I lie down to sleep you stand astride my forehead like a ladder stretching up between the stars, a geometric ladder or a beanstalk or a ladder where the dreams fly in and out like birds like leaves like birds until I wake and see your high red light. From there I look back down and see your feet receding, watch them turning clockwise through the eyes of someone younger stoned or drunk someone my age with inflammation of the middle ear – I see the whole dark world slip sideways as I try to walk away towards my what my midnight destiny my younger life my midnight – *Christ!* – before I have to stop and kneel at this ceramic bathroom fitting to throw up.

Sirinas

Above our heads, inside the plane tree's canopy of leaves
the shade is singing. It must be some artifice –
a speaker mounted somewhere, birdsong in a loop
left running. How else
could these few liquid trills and twitterings
fill up this whole green space?
Around us men talk quietly and lift their misted glasses
and replace them, barely raising their eyes
towards the hanging bamboo cages.

No money at the cashpoints. Underfoot
the schoolyard gravel glitters
mixed with broken glass, the panes unmended.
Two hundred kilometres to the south-south-east
the rafts are still arriving
overloaded – filled with men and women, children, eyes
searching the horizon – while we all alight
from Germany or England, or by car
from Eastern Europe, in our carefree crowds

to where we sit and listen to these birds
we try and fail to see, and feel our small hearts burst.

Reading Scott Fitzgerald at the Gorgona

To live again that sunlit snake of road
across the shoulder of the mountain
up through Panagía, down through pines
to Golden Beach, where groups of draggled bathers
trailing inflatables from their limp fingers
stand and blink as we edge slowly past –
then up to where the monastery
brandishes its fig leaves high above the sea,
past blackened inlets to this little promontory,
olive-grove intact. And here, this view. Just two
lone swimmers in the water, one with snorkel,
flippering face-down among the rocks.
Two others walking in the ruins,
towels across their shoulders, almost
could be us. Their life could be or could have been
our life. Too late. We're high above
the crash of waves, cicadas shrilling from each tree;
a scattering of rainbow clothes-pegs
glints between the leaves.

I close my eyes and see the girl who climbed
the H of Hollywood and jumped – no compromise
in those twin verticals! – and idly substitute
the H of Hughes and Heaney, all those lethal
Ls – for Lowell, Larkin, Longley – and the
Ooo! of Olds. How hard to drag her woman's weight
like that, alone beside the highway in the heat
or cold, her hands all smeared with dirt.
The P for Poetry or Plath might be unkind
and yet still possible. A T for Thomas you could
hang from, swinging, warning other travellers
of what they risked. An R you'd just about
slide down from. And an E?

The Y you learn to stay with – look, it offers you a hold
between two forking branches, where you find
the road retreating, covered by a mountain,
and this sunlit invitation
while you wait here in the parting of a question,
kicking your heels against the upright like a child.

Olive Tree with Clothes-pegs

It fills this dappled space
with its long leaves, dull green, grey-silver,
here and there already a trace of something
yellowing – and occupies the air
with a web of interlocking branches
delicate as wire, the greyed-out filaments
meeting and criss-crossing. Yet its messages
are scrambled: where I'm expecting grey
there's colour; where my pupils grow to meet the shade
a splash of light. Between the lowest twigs
the leaves are turning orange, red, the brilliant
green of spring and is it – yes! – bright blue. I blink
and start to make out lines of unseen cord
and count them – nine, all radiating from one trunk.
And, now my eyes have somehow learned to look
at olive trees, the shade is even deeper and the water
underneath us turquoise, while across the cove
the ruins lie like two millennia of fallen
chimneys in pale negative – and threaded through
between the washing-lines a trumpet vine
is rising, coiling, twisting like a flame
into the highest branches, where it re-emerges
in a blast of orange, waving
from the bole that someone's careful brush
has painted white for visitors like us
who saunter out to shoreline restaurants at dusk
to eat and no doubt drink and stumble half-asleep
uphill to this cool garden
where the two of us could wander, arms outstretched,
and lose ourselves in darkness. So it can be seen.

Leaving Alikí

How is it possible to leave
this gently surging water, these old walls

and broken columns lying on their sides?
The beachside restaurants

are all but empty, though their bulbs are lit
in welcome for – who knows.

In giant pots, the basil still luxuriates,
hibiscus pushes out its tongues;

a finger of moonlight on the water
touches the aluminium carcases of loungers,

masts that sway and clink
and almost meet each other, cross.

That many-coloured bird
which hangs above the counter at Leonidas

still swings inside its cage
emitting screeches like a smoke alarm

that reach you when you're swimming in the cove
and make you think of love.

Credo

Rounding the headland on our way back
we saw it standing sideways on a ledge of rock
above the waterline in a small cave, so still and delicate
it looked sculpted out of marble. *That's not real,*
you said. And I said, *Yes it is.* It turned its head
and seemed to see us. Goat.

After all these years I think you still believe
in saints enshrined in niches, subtle enough
to cheat the eye, the strands of stone
that mimic hair or fur, the lineaments of skeleton
and sinew – even now you find them miraculous. While I,
what is it I believe in? Here, from this small boat

on swaying water, if I can believe
in anything, it's something rank and warm and full of blood
that jumps from crag to crag
over the churning surf and turns its silly head
and leaps and risks a stumble – climbs and climbs
until it reaches what?

A narrow jut of rock
it surely can't escape from, but
somehow it can, it will, and yes, in fact
I do believe in this, in something never yet
enshrined or chiselled:
I believe in goat.

Sunset at Karnagio

Pregnant and in-your-face
in the briefest of bikinis, she was surely
eight months gone – just showing off
her body, what it was, what it could do
and what it held, as if to make us reassess
our own or shrink, embarrassed, stare at the horizon,
down into a glass. She lounged
on a day bed, stroking her taut globe
that gleamed above the manmade marble beach –
then stood and tossed her honey-coloured bob
and strutted her great self
against the waves. And ambled back,
a filmy beach wrap floating in the breeze
from her slim shoulders, with a shift of weight,
a smile. And only then
did we see the photographer half-crouched
among the beanbags, aiming his dark lens
into the future. Was it to advertise the bar,
the island or the state itself
of motherhood? Whatever magazine it was
it had 'tomorrow' in the title
and behind a screen of flesh
its voiceless subject slept,
lulled by the suck of water, the shingle's rush.

Marble Beach, with Crane

Even here your image follows us:
beside a cleft of milky, salty,
urine-saturated sea, a beach
augmented with white marble
and a beachside café with a bored DJ
who pipes his music
to a speaker inches from our ears.
Backdrop of mountains, with a blinding gash
of quarry, marble waste in piles
and white dirt roads. Yet even here
we find you, resting, folded
to a letter Z, anonymous.

What can we do now but wait
watching for the boat
to round the headland,
nose up to the dock
and moor against the squeaking tyres
to take us back?

Dear Crane,

They've left you this narrow strip of blue – enough for
a sailor's trousers. On this scrap, your beam points up
like scissors severing a thread, two threads, a remnant.
Quick, point up, point in, shear through, before the cloud
gap closes. Someone's patchwork heart is pinned in place.
Already cumulus is looming from the west, the rain unrolls
its ticking. Someone else's crumpled view is gathered up.

Dear Crane,

Sometimes I look across and see you on a bank of cloud, a storm somewhere, not here, not yet, but 'over Will's mother', as my old neighbour would have said. Out there as we speak a storm unfurls, the giant hailstones bounce on lichened roof tiles, skitter down the chimney, rattle in the hearth. The sky is black, then lightens, leaves a rainbow with a crock of water slimed by snails. Between the metal crisscross of your ribs we squint to see Will's mother, glimpse her distant village with its steeple, glint of weathervane in sun. Already she's moved on. She cries or laughs. She's lost without her son, who never comes to visit. We are here beside your concrete slab and she is somewhere else, she's at the rainbow's end. The only way to find her is to disappear.

Dear Crane,

Have you ever wondered what controls the cables of a human heart? How when it swings it sometimes swings too far and can't swing back, so everything it worked to build is lost? How every plan already has a draft of demolition in it, how the dust is settling even as you stand there in your yellowness? Your Yellowness, you only stand there and look down on us, while under you we wake and learn to crawl and walk and go to school and work until we're old and lose our faculties and stop, while you go on. Can't you hear us when we slap our foreheads, can't you even see us here below you scrolling through our smartphones iPads laptops, eyebrows raised in disbelief, all muttering *Good Crane!*

Dear Crane,

This sun that falls through herringbones of leaf is making
you recede – a thin metallic feather poking from a roof
as if from someone's hat. These arching canopies of gold
and palest green on green to almost black with pigeons
cooing through them leave you *what*? From where I sit,
half-lying in my deckchair, you look shrunken, unremark-
able, a joke! How can I have gazed at you for all these
months through autumn winter spring, and see you
come to this? In this great flowering, where roses spread
their petals, open their tight hearts to sunlight, all you
do is wait. Beneath you bees are travelling from one
head to the next. Our two remaining ash trees ripple in
the breeze, tell us they're still alive. But you in your great
wisdom, you're preparing us. You're leaving, imperceptibly
withdrawing into the dappled shadows, dwarfed by this
green edifice which lifts itself.

After a Daughter's Miscarriage

(Cove Park, September 2016)

If you wake early to leave home
while it's still dark, driving or being driven
along a winding road
where trees reach out and touch
and magpies – three of them, I counted –
hop and flutter on the tarmac,
and you're travelling by car and then by plane
through cloud to land in Glasgow, then by bus
where at an unexpected bend your case
decides to leave you on its own four wheels,
and then in stops and starts
by train to Gourock, where there's a sudden
rainbow so low-slung it almost lies
on the horizon, more a bow
and less an arch than any you have seen
and mirrored in the water –
then by boat that dips and bobs and sways
towards Kilgerran, finally
by pick-up here, where wind and rain
across the surface of a pond
swirl endlessly like someone blowing
on a bowl of soup
beyond the time of cooling, far beyond
the time of thirst or hunger
till the mouth that blew
has surely died and yet it still goes on
in silver, black, a sweeping cloud
of rain that dances forward, back,
a quickstep on the surface –

Then you tell yourself that no one really
knows if what is dead

is truly dead, or only practising
the way this rain, this quick-quick forward-back
retreats, collects itself, and hesitates,
prepares to come again.

The Road to Bardigues

(for Bridget)

That afternoon I left my life behind
and walked towards Bardigues
to where the pilgrim sign – a sun
emitting rays, or is it a fluted shell? –
invited me to take an unmade path
that curled around the edge of a ravine
fringed with young poplars, brambles,
fruit black and wizened on the stem –
remembering the morning years ago,
at the same crossroads in this little town
with you, when I'd come to say goodbye;
how you'd gone on alone
uphill, under your rucksack's weight,
these same white pebbles underfoot
and grass and yellowed leaves,
this same path threatening to climb
to where the trucks rush past
towards Toulouse. I stumble down
through arches daubed with messages,
come out the other side
as you did, then I turn and wander back –
and there above my head,
following the line of the horizon,
working a far field and towing
something I can't quite make out,
a tiny tractor creeps towards me like a
scaled-down revelation
such as a small god vouchsafes a human
who has walked the pilgrim path
barely a few hours in both directions.

On the Day of the Royal Wedding

(19 May 2018)

Walking all morning, along sunken paths
between banks of bluebells, ragged robin, primroses –

we miss our way and stop beside a churchyard,
open our blowing map, and with our index fingers

trace our route from one field to the next
to where we strike uphill around the corner of a farmhouse

into sunlight, past a square of rutted dirt
where someone's parked a tractor, leaving it driverless.

And it is praying. *Hallowed be Thy name,*
give us this day, forgive us: the words rise and float

free of the empty cab and up between the leaves
towards the edge of Exmoor. No one here but us

and this steep green, with ewes and three-month lambs
scattered across a hillside like grey stones –

until a man emerges, turns his still-warm key
in the ignition and the voice we heard

is drowned out by his engine as we walk away.

Lopped Trees

The plane trees have become their bones,
their swollen joints – passing
from summer to winter in an afternoon.

Each of them reaches a dozen arms,
shows us the flat of its hands.
No memory of green

except the half-imagined spaces
they now let in – the hedge, the shrubs,
the weed-choked water, the far bank,

its poplars radiating in a geometric fan
grown for the laths of crates.
Our world has turned itself half blue

with sky, the painted superstructure
of a bridge I can't not watch
them cart the severed limbs across.

Even the leaves have been swept up
barely wilted. And we are left
with water, sunlight, distances.

Windmill above Golfech

Between the rows of drying corn-stalks
and a white gravel road
it raises its dark cross, its wall
pocked by past rains. Its sails are skeletal,
each with a kind of elbow, each
framing a rise of sky
the way a ladder does. Below,
a man-size door, a single window
hardly taller than a child.

But on the sunlight-blinded screen of my phone
the sails are wings, transparent as a dragonfly's –
and at its feet down on the plain
the Golfech cooling-towers
proffer their wisp of vapour like a tongue.

Dear Crane,

At first we fail to notice anything has changed. It's only when we're walking back that I look up and see that where your see-through body used to stand there's only see-through, where your metal heart would dangle on a ground of cloud there's only cloud. Your slewing unit's slewed itself and gone. It's what you do – erase yourself, move on to where you're needed. Now no shadow of a tower falls across the roofs. Our sky is heartless, as it always was. The building's still unfinished, webbed in scaffolding. Its plastic sheeting flaps. Yet something glints – a new-glazed window finds the evening sun. The rest's for us to manage. Your work's done.

Dear Crane,

Weeks after you departed here you are – not you but other yous, in other scales and colours: here between the absent walls of the old hospital, or in the hairpin spaces of the streets above a foreign harbour. Here on wheels between containers where your name's Potain, Gottwald, Liebherr, or here at home, this diesel-crusted hangar haunted by dead buses, *sorry, not in service* in a passing band of light. The land's already sold, a poster prophesies your future coming. By December you could be on site, in motion, back to move another stack of bricks for yet another home for the retired a few blocks farther on. And then again you're gone. Each time we register your absence we are practising our own.

Dear Crane,

Think of what's meant by *tune* and try to hum its opposite
– a not-quite-jangle, not-quite-jarring-clank, a not-in-
sequence note then silence then another note, the two of
them not *meaning*, not consecutive, a song that's lost its
voice, its ear, its person. Not even tune exactly, just an
empty space that waits, its voiceless buzz at night when
nobody's awake. Call it a tune, or call it *nothing*, non-
phrase sounding endlessly through night until its hearers
die, the low metallic moan you've made these many
months, swinging from east to west, air playing through
your girders. Call it an *air*, the sound you'll make as
you move on. Steel band without a player, wind chimes
starved of wind, you'll never be soprano, tenor, bass.
You'll always be a growler, mouthing words in silence,
turning this way and that, pretending to vibrate.

The Sunday Hunters

Already in the grey of early morning
I hear their voices underneath our window
and when I open up the shutters
there are two men, sucking at cigarettes,
the thinner one retelling some old story
and the heavier pooh-poohing,
waving it away towards the river
sealed in mist, the water
swollen by a night of rain upstream. And then
the dogs all yapping, howling, straining
at their leashes, bundled into cars
in the gravel car park, and the engines
roaring to life, the noises fading,
till a silence spreads itself across the grass.
There's just the church bell clanging from its cliff,
a motorbike buzzing across the bridge.

Next morning when I push the shutters back
the men have gone, the river's in full sun
and the street outside is wet
as if hosed down, a giant patch of dark
where something wild lay dying
in a pool of blood, and was sliced up
and roasted on a spit and eaten
while they roared in triumph and their drunken
songs *et glou et glou* rolled echoing
under the rotting doors and up the slope
to where in beds of grass and trodden bracken
breathing bodies shivered momentarily awake,
their ears still pricked to listen
to the scrape of plates, the clink of glasses
and we almost heard them,
only a wall between us while we slept.

Robert Singing

Now, at night, the table is lit up
with wine and candles as he starts to sing:

Edith Piaf, and no regrets
although he's almost ninety; *Tosca*, and his voice

is not quite there, not quite
reaching the higher notes, not all it must have been, and yet

it's beautiful, its flaws are flaws we recognise,
there for a good reason – all of his past life and ours

are here with us. I find myself
smiling as he leans across the glasses, sings

as if for me, and Jamie wipes away a tear – and yes,
the young man that he was could surely sing

the hind legs off a donkey, and the old man that he is
can hold that young man in his larynx

and console him, touch him as he was.

Notes

Midwich Cuckoo (44)
Netherne was the name of the Surrey County Asylum at
Hooley.

Reading Scott Fitzgerald at the Gorgona (58)
The reference is, via Scott Fitzgerald, to the young Welsh
actress Peg Entwistle, who committed suicide in 1932.

The Sunday Hunters (78)
'*et glou et glou*' is from a French drinking song: translated
into English, the chorus is 'He is one of us: he has drunk
his wine like the others.'